D1317528

WHAT IS EARWAX MADE OF?

And Other FAQs About Your Body

By Kristen Rajczak Nelson

Gareth Stevens
PUBLISHING

Please visit our website, www.garethstevens.com. For a free color catalog of all our high-quality books, call toll free 1-800-542-2595 or fax 1-877-542-2596.

Library of Congress Cataloging-in-Publication Data

Names: Nelson, Kristen Rajczak.
Title: What is earwax made of? : and other FAQs about your body / Kristen
   Rajczak Nelson.
Description: New York : Gareth Stevens Publishing, [2017] | Series: Q & A:
   Life's mysteries solved! | Includes bibliographical references and index.
Identifiers: LCCN 2015045648 | ISBN 9781482447644 (pbk.) | ISBN 9781482447712 (library bound) | ISBN
9781482447682 (6 pack)
Subjects: LCSH: Earwax–Juvenile literature.
Classification: LCC RF190 .N45 2017 | DDC 617.8–dc23
LC record available at http://lccn.loc.gov/2015045648

Published in 2017 by
Gareth Stevens Publishing
111 East 14th Street, Suite 349
New York, NY 10003

Copyright © 2017 Gareth Stevens Publishing

Designer: Andrea Davison-Bartolotta
Editor: Kristen Nelson

Photo credits: Cover, p. 1 (boy) Philary/Vetta/Getty Images; cover, pp. 1 (doodle), 4, 11 (needle), 22 (doodles), 25 (spine) advent/Shutterstock.com; p. 5 Daniele Pietrobelli/Shutterstock.com; p. 6 (bottom) Christopher Rynio/Hemera/Thinkstock; p. 6 (top) heromen30/Shutterstock.com; p. 7 (bottom) Jose Luis Pelaez Inc/Blend Images/Getty Images; p. 7 (top) Eric Isselee/Shutterstock.com; p. 8 (brain) James Kopp/iStock/Thinkstock; p. 8 (thermometer) Netkoff/Shutterstock.com; p. 9 Piotr Marcinski/Shutterstock.com; p. 10 ChameleonsEye/ Shutterstock.com; p. 11 (main) KidStock/Blend Images/Getty Images; p. 12 FamVeld/Shutterstock.com; p. 13 (left) Tushchakorn/Shutterstock.com; p. 13 (right) Cultura RM Exclusive/PhotoStock-Isreal/Getty Images; p. 14 Pasieka/ Science Photo Library/Getty Images; p. 15 (kale) Yulia von Eisenstein/Shutterstock.com; p. 15 (milk) YuliaKotina/ Shutterstock.com; p. 15 (kefir) Viktor1/Shutterstock.com; p. 15 (spinach) Ekaterina Kondratova/ Shutterstock.com; p. 15 (arugula) yoshi0511/Shutterstock.com; p. 15 (cheese) Efired/Shutterstock.com; p. 15 (girl) Veronica Louro/Shutterstock.com; p. 16 (main) Patrick Foto/Shutterstock.com; pp. 16 (DNA), 28 (garbage) LHF Graphics/Shutterstock.com; p. 17 Fuse/Corbis/Getty Images; p. 18 Raphye Alexius/Blend Images/Getty Images; p. 19 Anup Shah/Digital Vision/Thinkstock; p. 20 motttive/Shutterstock.com; p. 21 (bottom) Sabina Zak/ Shutterstock.com; p. 21 (top) Milkovasa/Shutterstock.com; p. 22 (main) bikeriderlondon/Shutterstock.com; p. 23 (main) Hank Morgan/Science Source/Getty Images; p. 23 (inset) Photo Researchers/Science Source/Getty Images; p. 24 Tomacco/Shutterstock.com; p. 25 (wisdom teeth) Sebastian Kaulitzki/Shutterstock.com; p. 25 (foot) LeventeGyori/Shutterstock.com; p. 26 structuresxx/Shutterstock.com; p. 27 (inset) courtesy of NASA; p. 27 (main) ESA/Handout/Getty Images; p. 28 (nose) Studio_smile/Shutterstock.com; p. 28 (smile) grmarc/Shutterstock.com; p. 28 (boy) Sudowoodo/Shutterstock.com; p. 28 (pool) Kateryna Mostova/Shutterstock.com; p. 29 (boy) michaeljung/Shutterstock.com; p. 29 (man silhouette) Vector Goddess/Shutterstock.com; p. 29 (heart) oxanaart/ Shutterstock.com; p. 29 (small intestine texture) Mopic/Shutterstock.com.

Printed in the United States of America

CPSIA compliance information: Batch #CS16GS: For further information contact Gareth Stevens, New York, New York at 1-800-542-2595.

Contents

Words in the glossary appear in **bold** type the first time they are used in the text.

BODY TALK

Your body is amazing! It can heal, fight illness, run, and more. But how does it do all this and still get itchy, sticky, and sweaty? The answers you seek—and some you didn't even know you sought—can be found within the pages of this book!

Q: What is earwax made of?

A: The scientific word for earwax is cerumen (suh-ROO-muhn). It's a pretty gross combination of things: sebum (fatty matter made by the skin), dead skin from inside the ear, and other **secretions** from the outer ear canal. Most of the time, earwax cleans up after itself, so you don't have to deal with it. Whenever you chew or move your jaw, your earwax moves slowly from the eardrum to the opening of your ear. There it can dry and fall out.

Don't do this! Earwax should come out on its own.

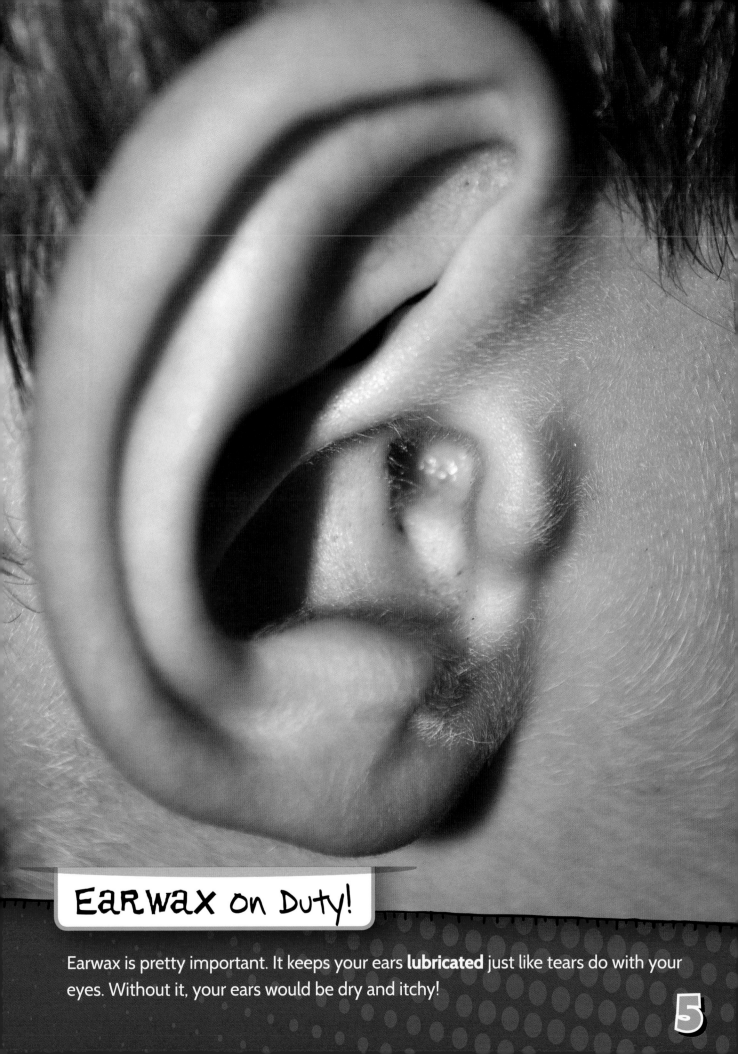

Earwax on Duty!

Earwax is pretty important. It keeps your ears **lubricated** just like tears do with your eyes. Without it, your ears would be dry and itchy!

Q: Is my hair alive?

A: Yes and no. The part of the hair under your skin, including the root, is alive. The root grows inside a **follicle** and is fed by tiny blood vessels at its base. By the time hair becomes something you can see, such as eyebrows or the hair you brush in the morning (or not), it's made of dead cells.

FOLLICLE

Have you ever been scared enough for your hair to stand up? Like other **mammals**, humans used to make their hair stand up to look bigger to predators.

You have hair all over your body, or almost. The only parts of your body that don't have hair are your lips, the palms of your hands, and the soles of your feet. Much of the hair on your body is very light and hard to see. It wasn't always that way. Human **ancestors** used to have protective fur, much like chimpanzees!

No Way!
People have the same number of hairs on their body as chimpanzees do.

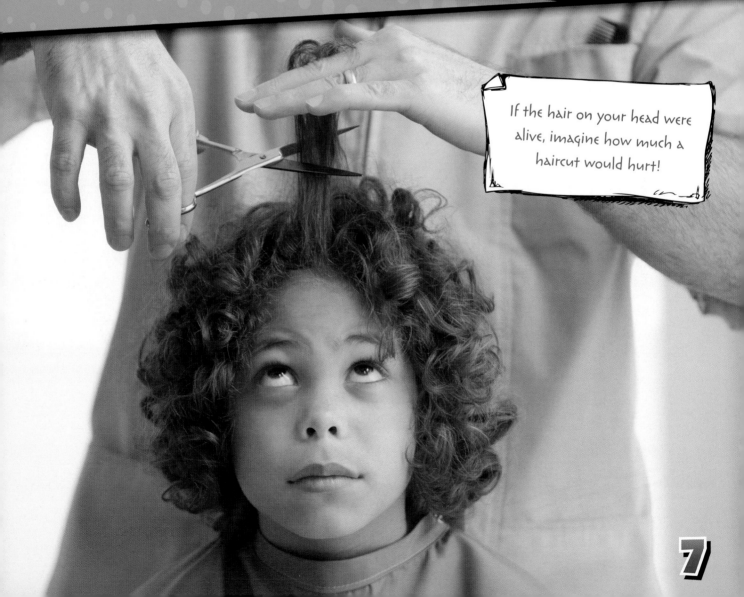

If the hair on your head were alive, imagine how much a haircut would hurt!

Q: Why do I get a fever when I'm sick?

A: Fevers serve two important purposes. First, the higher body temperature makes your body a less welcoming place for germs! Second, it lets you—and your mom or doctor—know that you're sick so you know to rest and take medicine.

The hypothalamus is the part of the brain that keeps your body temperature at about 98.6°F (37°C). When germs start to grow in your body, chemicals in your blood let the hypothalamus know it's time to crank up the heat!

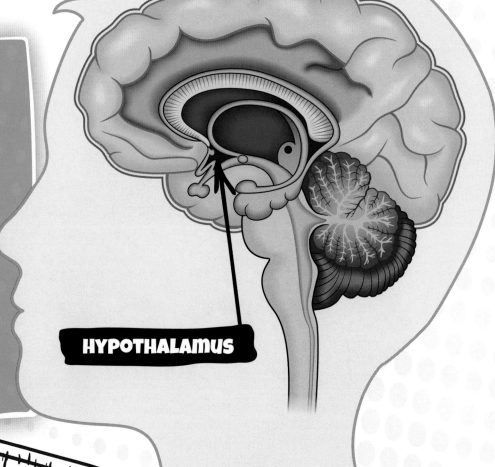

HYPOTHALAMUS

Q: Can I catch a cold from being outside in cold weather?

A: Technically no, cold weather doesn't cause a cold, a virus does. But recent **research** suggests that when your body temperature falls, your body doesn't fight a cold virus as well. The study showing this was done on mice, which means it's not 100 percent sure that the response will be the same in people. But to be safe, you should probably wear a coat in winter weather.

The air from your sneeze may move at 100 miles (160 km) per hour!

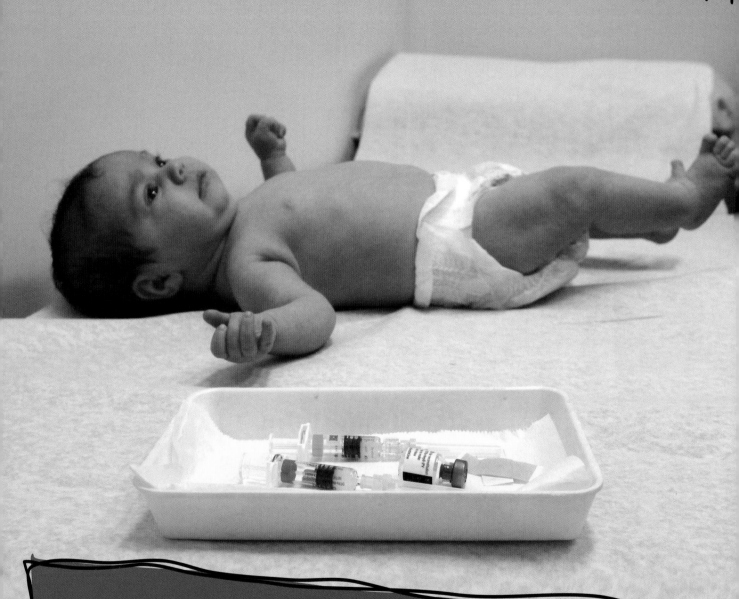

Do you hate getting shots? You probably don't even remember getting the most important shots of your life! When you were a baby, you may have gotten a series of vaccinations for diseases that could cause serious problems as you grow up. Some of these diseases, such as polio, used to cause many deaths and now rarely happen in the United States!

A Vaccine Won't Make You Sick

Choosing to put a dead or weak illness in your body doesn't give you **symptoms** of that disease. However, after getting a vaccination, your arm might hurt or be a little red. Some people might get a slight fever, but truly bad **reactions** to a vaccine are very rare. Getting the right vaccines will protect you from many illnesses—and keep you from passing a disease to those around you!

Vaccines are shots that can save your life!

Q: Do babies have more bones than adults?

A: Yes! A baby has 300 bones when it's born, but an adult has 206. Why is that? All bones start as cartilage, a soft **tissue**. While some body parts, such as your ear, will always be made of cartilage, others become bones, or ossify, over time. Babies have some bones when they're born, but they have many cartilage parts that ossify as they grow. Many bones also fuse, or grow together, until babies have an adult skeleton! For example, babies' skulls are made of three big plates when they're born, and the plates fuse to make one bone!

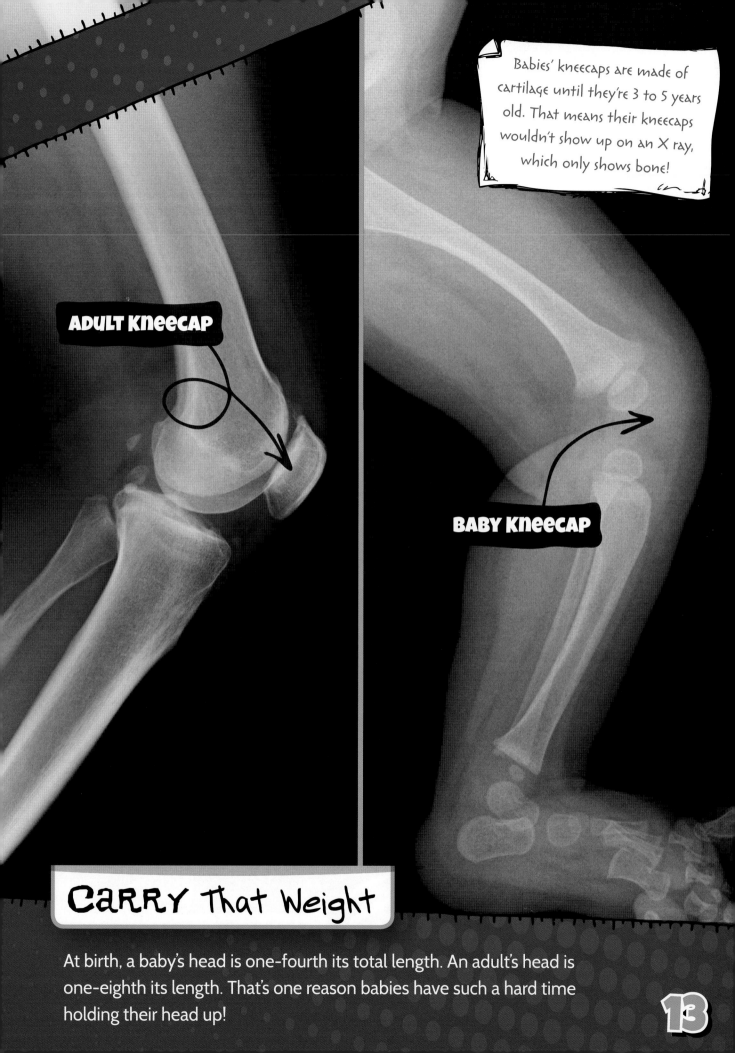

ADULT KNEECAP

Babies' kneecaps are made of cartilage until they're 3 to 5 years old. That means their kneecaps wouldn't show up on an X ray, which only shows bone!

BABY KNEECAP

CaRRY That Weight

At birth, a baby's head is one-fourth its total length. An adult's head is one-eighth its length. That's one reason babies have such a hard time holding their head up!

Q: Why do old people seem to shrink?

A: Over many years, older people *do* become shorter! Gravity causes the disks between the bones in the spine to become compressed as the years go by. Osteoporosis is another reason. This condition causes bones to break down, and the body doesn't create enough new bone. Shrinking is a long process and can be slowed by exercising and eating healthfully. Foods with lots of calcium, such as milk and green leafy vegetables, keep your bones especially healthy.

Eating a well-balanced diet now can help your bone health when you're older!

HEALTHY SPINE

SPINE WITH OSTEOPOROSIS

Calcium-Rich Foods

leafy vegetables

kale
collard greens
spinach
arugula
turnip greens

dairy products

milk
yogurt
kefir
cheese
cottage cheese

kale

milk

arugula

kefir

spinach

cheese

YOU Shrink, too!

Don't be afraid! Kids don't usually have osteoporosis to worry about yet (but you'd better eat some yogurt to be sure). However, by the time you go to bed at night, you're just a little shorter than you were when you woke up. That's gravity working again!

YOUR PARENTS ARE responsible for how you look.

Have you ever heard that you look *just like* your mom or dad? Hair color, eye color, height, and body type can all be traced to your genes. Half a child's genes come from their father and half from their mother. Of course, they don't get to choose which genes they pass on.

MOTHER/DAUGHTER SIDE BY SIDE

EXPRESS Yourself!

Having a gene isn't enough. It needs to be "turned on" to affect your appearance. Epigenetics are what's going on in your DNA outside of your genes. Genes are turned on and off, or used with other genes to make sure your body does things it should.

For a long time, scientists thought **identical** twins had the exact same genes, which is why they look so much alike! However, a new study has shown there actually can be differences in identical twins' genes.

Q: How does someone become left-handed?

A: About 10 percent of people are born left-handed. Genes control handedness, or the use of one hand more than the other. That's another thing you can blame on your parents! However, your upbringing plays a part, too. Most tools, such as scissors, are made for righties. And, in history, lefties were looked down on and sometimes forced to change.

- In medieval times, a left-handed person was thought to be possessed by the devil!

- In the Middle East, Africa, and India, the left hand is historically the "dirty" hand.

- The word "left" comes from the word "lyft," meaning "broken."

- "Weird," "incorrect," and "wrong" are all synonyms for "left" in Mandarin.

Poor lefties!

NOT Outnumbered Everywhere

In the animal kingdom, polar bears and chimpanzees have handedness, too. But they're more evenly split between righties and lefties. Chimpanzees are close to 50 percent left-handed!

Q: What makes people snore?

A: That snorting, grunting, or gargling sound your brother makes when asleep is called snoring. The sound is caused when air moves past something, like relaxed tissue, partly blocking the throat. Snoring is the **vibration** of these relaxed tissues during breathing. Snoring can be caused by the shape of a person's mouth and throat or tissue between the **nostrils** that isn't straight. People who have a cold often snore because their airway is blocked, too.

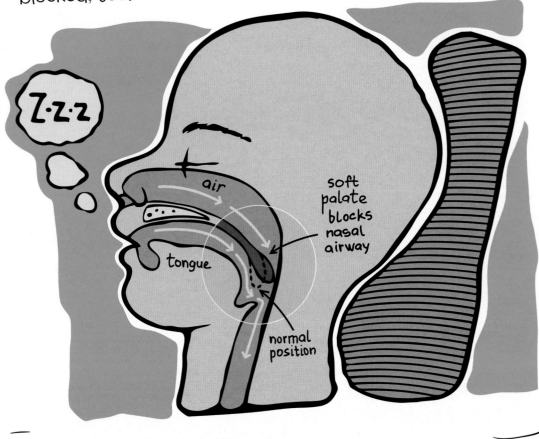

Z·z·z

air

tongue

soft palate blocks nasal airway

normal position

Snoring is commonly worst when the snorer is sleeping on their back. Gravity makes their throat even more relaxed!

About 60 percent of men and 40 percent of women will snore by age 60. These sounds are about 60 **decibels** on average, which is about the volume of someone speaking normally. Sometimes it seems a lot louder, though. Snores can reach more than 80 decibels! That's as loud as the drills used to break up concrete.

21

Q: Why do I need sleep?

A: Though sleeping seems to us to be a time for rest, so much is happening in your body as you sleep.

In the brain

Scientists believe that when you're asleep, your brain works through what you've learned that day and stores it. This is the time any waste is cleared out of the brain, too.

In the muscles

Do you play a sport? Sleep is the time your body repairs the tissue you have broken down by exercising. It helps you get stronger!

Get to bed On Time!

Kids ages 5 to 12 should be getting 10 to 11 hours of sleep a night! This will help you focus better in school, feel happier, and be able to remember things more easily.

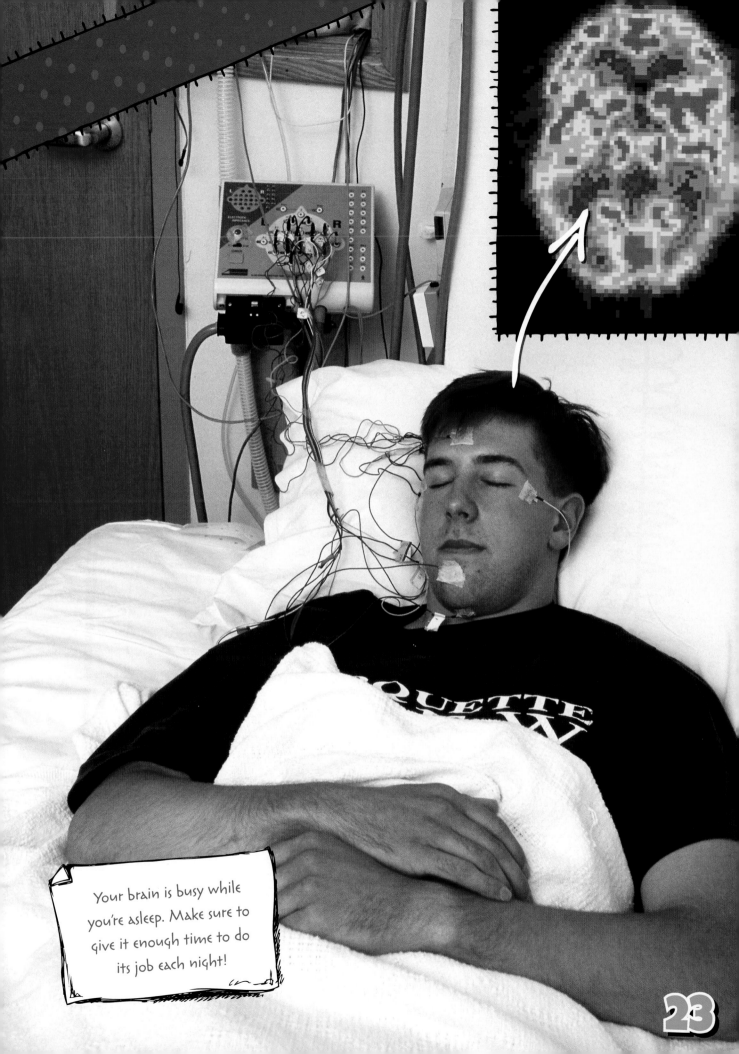

Your brain is busy while you're asleep. Make sure to give it enough time to do its job each night!

Q: Is the appendix really good for nothing?

A: No! Scientists have recently found that the appendix, a tiny **organ** in the lower right of your **abdomen**, helps the bacteria in your digestive system do their job. But if it gets infected and you need it taken out, those millions of little gut bacteria will still be just fine.

appendix

Wait...MILLIONS?

Yes! By count, your body contains more bacteria than human cells. About 32 million live on your skin, but many live in your stomach and small intestine to help you digest, or break down, food.

Other Useless Body Parts

wisdom teeth: Human ancestors once needed more wide, flat teeth to chew plants. Today, most people get these removed because they grow in wrong.

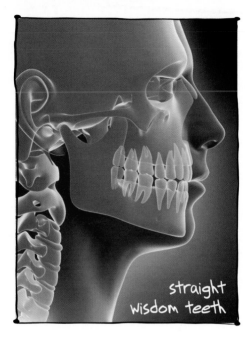

straight wisdom teeth

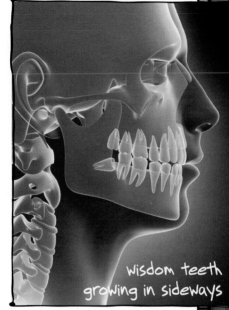

wisdom teeth growing in sideways

fifth toe: Is your "baby" toe tiny? It used to help people balance, but now the big toe has almost completely taken over that job.

coccyx: Made up of fused parts of **vertebrae**, this is what's left of the human tail! It was used for balance.

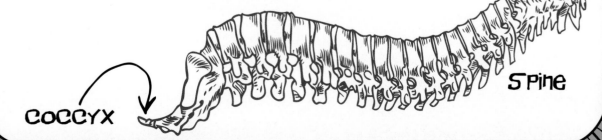

coccyx

spine

Q: What happens to your body in space without a space suit?

A: Without the air pressure of Earth's atmosphere, the air in your body would **expand**, and the water under your skin would turn to vapor. All that would make you almost twice your size—and really hurt! Your number one worry would be lack of air. After about 15 seconds, all the oxygen in your blood would be used up. If you were rescued within about a minute, you'd probably survive. Any longer, and you'd be dead of asphyxiation, or a lack of oxygen.

Wear a Space Suit!

Astronauts' space suits keep the correct pressure around their body, as well as keep them warm in cold, cold space. The suit also protects astronauts from the radiation, or energy, of the sun. Without one, you wouldn't live long enough to worry about cold or radiation!

HARD UPPER TORSO

(inside suit)

PRIMARY LIFE SUPPORT SYSTEM

HELMET

CAMERA

ARMS

LOWER TORSO ASSEMBLY

UPPER TORSO

GLOVES

The human nose can smell 50,000 different scents.

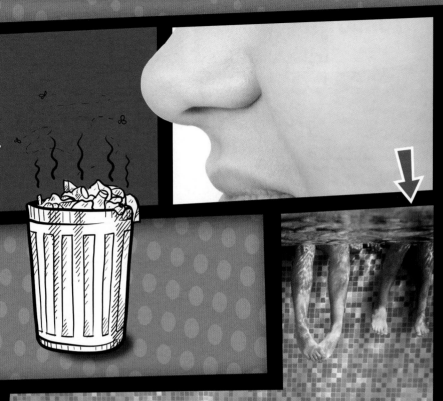

In your lifetime, you'll produce about 25,000 quarts (23,660 L) of spit, about two swimming pools' worth!

Most people have about 10,000 taste buds. About every 2 weeks, you get new ones!

In your body, there are about 60,000 miles (96,560 km) of blood vessels, if you laid them end to end.

Your heart pumps about 2,000 gallons (7,570 L) of blood through your body each day.

!! Wow your friends and family with some weird, cool, and gross facts about the human body! !!

18 FEET

The average person's small intestine is 18 to 23 feet (5.5 to 7 m) long.

6 FEET

People with blonde hair have about 146,000 hair follicles, while those with red hair have about 86,000 follicles. Those with black and brown hair have around 100,000 to 110,000 follicles.

Glossary

abdomen: the part of the body that contains the stomach

ancestor: someone who comes before others in a family

decibel: a unit used to measure loudness

expand: to get larger and looser

follicle: a small opening from which a hair grows

identical: being the same

lubricate: to make wet or slippery

mammal: a warm-blooded animal that has a backbone and hair, breathes air, and feeds milk to its young

microorganism: a tiny living thing, such as bacteria, that can only be seen with a microscope

nostril: an opening through which an animal breathes

organ: a part inside an animal's body

reaction: a response

research: studying to find something new

secretion: the product of a living thing that's given off to perform a specific useful function in the living thing

symptom: a sign that shows someone is sick

tissue: matter that forms the parts of living things

vertebrae: the small bones that make up the backbone

vibration: a rapid movement back and forth

BOOKS

Canavan, Thomas. *How Your Body Works: The Ultimate Illustrated Guide.* Mineola, NY: Dover Publications, Inc., 2015.

Shulman, Mark. *X Why Z: Your Body.* New York, NY: Time for Kids Books, 2015.

Zuchora-Walske, Christine. *Your Head Shape Reveals Your Personality! Science's Biggest Mistakes About the Human Body.* Minneapolis, MN: Lerner Publications Company, 2015.

WEBSITES

The Brain
coolkidfacts.com/facts-about-the-brain-for-kids/
Want to know more about the amazing brain? Visit this website for kids!

Human Body Facts
sciencekids.co.nz/sciencefacts/humanbody.html
Discover more cool facts about the human body, and find many links to even more information!

Index